HOW COLD IS IT?

Roger Welsch and Paul Fell

HOW COLD IS IT?

Roger Welsch and Paul Fell

ISBN 0-934904-34-0

987654321 9697989900

Published by

J&LLeeCo.
P.O. Box 5575
Lincoln, Nebraska 68505

Introduction by Roger Welsch

How cold is it? Well, it's been cold enough often enough to generate a blizzard of cold weather tall tales, that's for sure. America has always had a love affair with the tall tale, and that's not surprising. This is a tall-tale country, after all. But while it's hot in Florida, cold in Maine, windy in Chicago, wet in Seattle, the plain fact is, it's the Plains where it's hotter and colder, windier, wetter, bigger, smaller, better and worse than anywhere else. And if the statistics don't bear up under scrutiny . . . ? Well, as Jim Bridger, the great frontiersman once said, "If they don't understand what it means to wrestle a grizzly bear single-handed . . . just throw in another grizzly bear!"

Yessir, this is a landscape where "averages" don't generate much interest. For one thing, America's Great Plains are still in their adolescence. Most Plains states aren't much older than a single century, and while that may seem like a long time, it hasn't even been long enough to figure out exactly what the weather is like out here. That's why there are new records, high and low, fast and big, most and least, set out here almost on a weekly basis.

I like to think of the tall tale as a form of reverse bragging. Listen to one of those veteran liars holding court in a small-town tavern or a city barber shop . . . he may be talking about how miserable the weather is and how tough times are and how poor folks are around here and how mean the dogs are . . . but look at his face. Is he really complaining? I don't think so. Look closer. Isn't that just a wisp of a smile? And if things are so tough, why doesn't he go somewhere else? Because he loves it here, that's why. He loves this weather and this landscape and these people.

In effect, what he is saying is, "This place is so damned tough, no one but the toughest old coot alive could possibly survive in a miserable place like this. I'm doing fine."

I love this place too. Nice days are nice, sure, but what I relish are those Nebraska winters when the snow piles up so high I have to fight our way out of the farmyard with a tractor or walk up to town wearing show shoes. I like it when it's so cold my nose hairs freeze, the trees pop, and the river freezes solid. I like it when it's so cold I can walk into Eric's Tavern up in town and everyone grins that Plains grin and asks the inevitable, "Cold enough for you?"

I love that kind of winter day because then I can look around, pound the snow off my coat, wipe the ice off my nose, and ask back, "Cold? I didn't even notice. It's cold? How cold is it?"

Yes, indeed—HOW COLD IS IT?

IT WAS SO COLD
SOUNDS FROZE...

WE HAD TO THAW
OUT
CONVERSATIONS IN
A FRYING PAN...

WE FOUND A ROOSTER ALMOST DEAD...

A FOOT OF FROZEN CROW STICKING OUT OF HIS MOUTH...

FOR ALL THE ROOSTER CROWS AND TRAIN WHISTLES THAWING OUT.

I SAW TWO COTTONTAILS PUSHING A
JACKRABBIT...

JUST TO GET HIM STARTED!

I WAS STUCK BETWEEN THE BARN AND THE HOUSE...

FOLKS WORE SANDPAPER UNDERWEAR...

OUR RED PICKUP TRUCK TURNED BLUE!

I FOUND A DOG FROZEN TO THE FRONT TIRE OF MY CAR!

FOR A QUARTER
HOUR I WAS JUST
SHAKING HANDS
WITH MYSELF...

MILK FROZE BEFORE
IT HIT THE BOTTOM
OF THE BUCKET...

SO I JUST MILKED
OUT OVER MY LEFT
ARM...

AND WHEN I HAD A
BUNDLE OF FROZEN
SQUIRTS

I TIED IT WITH
BINDER TWINE AND
STACKED IT IN THE
BARN LOFT...

WHEN MOM WAS
COOKING,

SHE'D JUST SEND US
OUT FOR HOWEVER
MANY SQUIRTS HER
RECIPE CALLED FOR.

SOME FARMERS
JACKED UP THEIR
COWS...

AND BROKE OFF
THE MILK WITH A
STICK.

THERE WERE
DAIRIES THAT SOLD
MILK BY THE FOOT

EVENTUALLY OUR
COWS GAVE
NOTHING BUT ICE
CREAM.

THE FLAME FROZE
ON THE LANTERN
WICKS...

WE COULDN'T BLOW
THEM OUT SO WE
COULD GET SOME
SLEEP...

SO WE BROKE THEM
OFF, THREW THEM
OUTDOORS...

CHICKENS ATE
THEM...

AND THE TEETH ON MY BUZZ SAW WERE CHATTERING.

I HAD TO USE JUMPER CABLES TO GET MY WHEELBARROW STARTED.

WE WARMED UP THE HOUSE BY TURNING THE REFRIGERATOR ON DEFROST AND LEAVING THE DOOR OPEN.

AN ICE FLOE IN THE CREEK BY OUR PLACE HAD A POLAR BEAR ON IT.

AND IF THE
BOTTOM HAD
BEEN THREE
INCHES
LONGER...

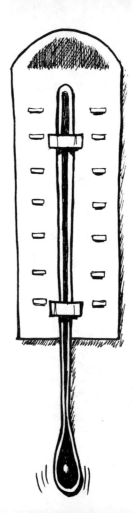

WE WOULD
HAVE FROZEN
TO DEATH...

ONE NEIGHBOR
HAD TO DIG
THREE FEET
INTO THE
FROZEN
GROUND...

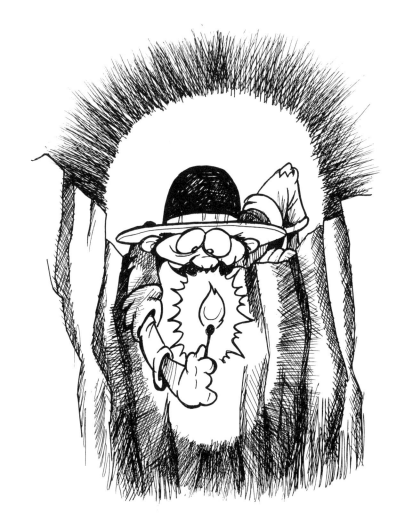

JUST TO READ
THE
TEMPERATURE ON
HIS
THERMOMETER...

WE SAVED OUR
LIVES BY PUTTING
OUR
THERMOMETER IN
BOILING WATER...

SO IT WAS SOON 110° IN THE SHADE.

MA'S TEETH CHATTERED ALL NIGHT...

OUR OVEN DOOR FROZE SHUT...

AND THE BISCUITS BURNED!

I WENT TO GET SOME WHISKEY TO KEEP ME WARM...

BUT IT HAD FROZEN...

SO THE BARTENDER CHIPPED OFF A HUNK...

AND I CARRIED IT HOME IN A HANDKERCHIEF.

WE TRIED ICE FISHING BUT CHOPPING A HOLE
FOR OUR BOAT WAS TOO MUCH TROUBLE...

BUT WHEN WE FINALLY DID GET THE JOB
DONE...

WE CAUGHT ALMOST 200 POUNDS OF ICE!

UNDERTAKERS HAD TO POUND CLIENTS INTO THE GROUND WITH A PILE DRIVER.

I LOOKED OUT AT OUR BIRD FEEDER THIS MORNING...

AND SAW A PENGUIN.

I SAW TWO GUYS SMOKING CIGARS...

I WAS NINE YEARS OLD...

BEFORE I KNEW CATS HAD EARS.

INDOOR CAT

OUTDOOR CAT

AND FROZE TO
DEATH ON THE
SPOT...

WE DRANK TABASCO MALTS JUST TO STAY WARM.

WE HAD TO GET ON THE ROOF AND CHOP CLOUDS OF FROZEN SMOKE OFF THE CHIMNEY...

WHICH WE THEN STORED IN THE ICE HOUSE...

AND USED THE NEXT SPRING TO SMOKE HAMS.

THE KITCHEN FLOOR WAS LITTERED WITH CHUNKS OF STEAM FROM THE TEAPOT SPOUT.

AND THEY WERE ESKIMOS!

OUR FURNACE DIED, SO I HEATED UP THE SHOP WITH A WOOD STOVE...

AND THEN EVERY SO OFTEN CARRIED A
GUNNY SACK FULL OF WARM INTO THE HOUSE.

OUR TOWN'S SNOW REMOVAL PROGRAM WAS CALLED "JULY".

WE THOUGHT WE WERE BLESSED, THOUGH...

WE COUNT ON WINTER TO FIX LEAKS IN OUR TRACTOR RADIATORS...

WE COULDN'T FIGURE OUT WHY OUR HOUSE
WAS SO COLD...

UNTIL WE WENT OUTSIDE AND FOUND THE ICICLES ON THE HOUSE HAD GROWN SO LONG...

THEY HAD LIFTED THE ROOF RIGHT OFF THE WALL!

OUR CROPS ARE SNOW PEAS, ICEBERG LETTUCE, ARCTICHOKES, AND NORTH POLE BEANS.

ACTUALLY, IT'S NOT THE WINTERS THAT ARE SO MISERABLE...

Other Books of Great Plains Interest

Nebraska, Where Dreams Grow. The fourth printing of Dorothy Weyer Creigh's 160-page paperback on Nebraska reminiscences from sodhouses and chautauqua to center-pivot irrigation. A delightful history of Nebraska told in terms of what people did in their everyday lives.   8½" x 11"   156 pages   15-4 $12.95

In All Its Fury. The story of the Great Blizzard of 1888. This storm, which covered nearly a third of the nation, roared down from Canada at 50 miles an hour, dropped temperatures 36 degrees, and killed more than 1,000 people, is described through the eyes of survivors. These accounts of heroism and courage were collected by W.H. O'Gara of Laurel, Nebraska, in 1947.   9" x 6"   343 pages   04-9 $9.95

Sod Walls. The sod house has gone from being one of the most common dwellings in Nebraska to the point where only a few originals still stand. Great Plains folklorist Roger Welsch has told the story of soddies in over 100 photos and illustrations with a clear and interesting text.   6" x 8"   208 pages   27-8 $12.95

Pinnacle Jake + Pinnacle Jake's Roundup. As told to Nellie Snyder Yost. 84 years worth of vivid recollections from A. B. "Pinnacle Jake" Snyder on what cowboy life was really like at the turn of the century. J. Frank Dobie said it is "one of the best range books I have read . . ." Includes nearly 100 pages of new – never before published – pages of Great Plains range life tales.   8" x 5"   340 pages   28-6 $12.95

Oh Grandma, You're Kidding. Gladys Douglass recounts eighty years of memories of growing up in Nebraska, told in humorous and interesting detail. Covering everyday life in the Great Plains and how it was survived. 30 chapters include: Before TV and Radio; Woman's Work; Baked Beans on Washday; Riding the Train; Dollar Day At The Fair; Omaha's Easter Tornado; and Seeing Halley's Comet. A fascinating recounting for those who "remember when" or those unable to recall life before TV.   110 pages   00-6 $7.95

Seems Like Old Times; The Big Bands of the Midwest. From 1935 to 1955 the midwest was home to dozens of small traveling dance bands. Vocalist, band member and director Loren Belker recounts how these regional groups came about, lived and became a part of the midwest scene in a fascinating format filled with dozens of photographs.   8½" x 11"   131 pages   30-8 $16.95

Remember When. Over 100 vignettes of Lincoln history from Jim McKee's Lincoln *Journal* "Memories & Moments" column, collected with illustrations.   8½" x 5½"   202 pages   23-5

Luther North, Frontier Scout. Jeff O'Donnell. The scouts, who made the frontier railroads and settlement possible, were "one of the most thrilling chapters of Nebraska history." The story of Luther North, as told here, was one of the most fascinating links in the winning of the west.   10-3 $13.95

Lincoln: The Prairie Capital. This 124-page book by Jim McKee tells the history of Nebraska's capital city with interesting accounts, stories and hundreds of photos. McKee recounts Lincoln's past from the tiny village of 30 with "no water power, mines, fuel, nor other so-called natural advantages" to the modern city of nearly 180,000, punctuating historical facts and formalities with how-it-happened anecdotes.   8½" x 11"   124 pages   07-3 $17.95